A TAXI TO THE FLAME

THE
James
DICKEY
CONTEMPORARY POETRY SERIES

EDITED BY RICHARD HOWARD

A TAXI TO THE FLAME

POEMS BY

Vickie Karp

University of South Carolina Press

Published in Columbia, South Carolina, by the
University of South Carolina Press

Manufactured in the United States of America

03 02 01 00 99   5 4 3 2 1

Library of Congress Cataloging-in-Publication Data

Karp, Vickie.
    A taxi to the flame : poems / by Vickie Karp.
        p.   cm. — (The James Dickey contemporary poetry series)

    ISBN 1-57003-295-5 (alk. paper)
    ISBN 1-57003-296-3 (pbk. : alk. paper)
    I. Title.   II. Series.
    PS3561.A6923 T39   1999
    811'.54—ddc21   98-58075

The author offers grateful acknowledgments to the editors of the following publications, in which poems in this book originally appeared, sometimes in slightly different form: *Antioch Review,* "The Consequences of Waking"; *Canto,* "The Lost Lover"; *Esquire,* "Boat," "Winter and Its Steps"; *New Republic,* "One Hundred Well-Cut Leaves," "Places You'll Never Go"; *New York Review of Books,* "How Peace, after Asking Its Question, Becomes War," "Getting Dressed in the Dark"; *New York Times,* "Spark"; *New Yorker,* "Driving Home," "Dust," "Elegy," "Endless Greetings," "Glass," "Goodbye," "Harm," "The Neighborhood Environmental Center," "On Your Birthday, Looking through a Telescope at Jupiter," "Police Sift New Clues in Search for Beauty," "The Red Dress," "Sitting on the Beach with Nachman," "Stars," "Still Life in the Coat Factory Office," and "Tulips: A Selected History"; *Paris Review,* "The Juniper Bonsai"; *Parnassus,* "On the Satin Virtues of Milk"; *Poetry* (Hong Kong), "Driving Home"; *Texas Review,* "Insurance," "Tied to the Earth"; *Yale Review,* "A Taxi to the Flame," "Watching the Commuters Read." "Elegy" also appeared in *The Best Poetry of 1991* (Scribner's, 1991), and "Getting Dressed in the Dark" also appeared in *The Best Poetry of 1989* (Scribner's, 1989). "Glass," "Goodbye," and "The Neighborhood Environmental Center" also appeared in *Under 35: The New Generation of American Poets* (Doubleday, 1989). "The Consequences of Waking," "Still Life in the Coat Factory Office," and "A Taxi to the Flame" also appeared in *Walk on the Wild Side: Urban American Poetry since 1975* (Macmillan, 1994).

The author is grateful to the National Endowment for the Arts for a 1994 poetry grant and the New York Foundation for the Arts for a 1981 poetry grant.

Publication of this book was supported by a grant from the Eric Matthieu King Fund of The Academy of American Poets.

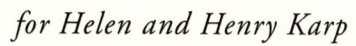

for Helen and Henry Karp

Contents

A Note on Vickie Karp

There is a kind of thinking, or of knowing—of *cognizance,* to sweep the two together—which proceeds, when it comes to expressive endeavors, by the recognition of objects, by the discovery of circumstances, by the awareness of situations, in terms of their resemblances and analogies to *other* objects, circumstances, situations. Such cognizance we call metaphor or trope, and we correct it, when its excesses are beyond us, by the idiot rehearsals we call identity. For these are the only instruments we have, metaphor and identity, with which to account for how the world strikes us, and in the enterprise of poets there are varying degrees, diverse densities of the one or the other. Of course words themselves are metaphors in some stage of decrepitude, so that even the austerest poet of identity is discovered to be metaphorical *deep down.* Perhaps because we do not choose to read that far down, we tend to accuse the poets of identity of a certain poverty, a certain bleakness—what Yeats called (and acclaimed as) *the desolation of reality.* On the other hand, we tend to accuse the poets of metaphorical richness of a certain confusion, a certain derangement; Shakespeare is *hard to read* if we are not trained to metaphorical cognizance. Though I wonder how hard . . . When Antony complains about "the hearts that spanieled me at heels," it seems to afford the (presumably untrained) playgoer no trouble at all to understand the trope even as the syllables flicker past. I guess the trouble begins as the out-of-favor warrior continues his complaint:

. . . The hearts
That spanieled me at heels, to whom I gave
Their wishes, do discandy, melt their sweets
On blossoming Caesar; and this pine is barked,
That overtopped them all. Betrayed I am . . .

Thick and fast the metaphors arrive—the spanieling hearts turn into dissolving confections which then, disconcertingly, somehow offer their delights to a rival Caesar perceived to be in flower, which flourishing at once summons the contrasting figure of a stripped fir that once towered over "them" (no longer hearts but Romans). Incidentally, there is no record of either verb, *to spaniel* or *to discandy,* occurring anywhere in our language except on these sole occasions in Shakespeare, whose capacity to trope finds no obstacle in the *hapax legomenon,* a verbal form used but once.

Of course this is all very well for Shakespeare . . . (if it is). But when a contemporary poet invests in such creative behaviors, contemporary readers may repine, and that is where I should like to intercede in Vickie Karp's behalf. This poet thinks metaphorically, with a Shakespearean luxuriance, and may, as in "Getting Dressed in the Dark," disconcert:

> . . . The body rises, shifting its inner tropic from swamp to tree,
> Pats the floor for its shoes, places a thumb
>
> On each side of a sock—the mugging grin of a boy
> About to stick out his tongue—
>
> And slowly, as if dipping a foot into cold water,
> Rolls the puddle up over each ankle.

Such metaphorical cognizance is endemic in Vickie Karp, and as a post-Shakespearean reader I revel in it, though I concede that you may need to give some time and attention to the exactitude of this poet's expression before you join her on the other side of consciousness. Of course what makes her the distinguished writer she is, the poet of responsible delight, is her awareness of this rare plenitude; she has a remarkable capacity to switch into a diction of great plainness, a lingo of what Shakespeare calls *the self-same,* which balances her poems wonderfully between the figural and the literal, between economy and extravagance, as in "Endless Greetings," her apostrophe to Monet which I believe to be her masterpiece, from which I cite the last six lines:

> Now a green smoke rises.
> An underwater bursts up and spreads its mackerel skin.
> The white rings of birch spin in solitude.
> The fragrance of the bank infuses the anticipation

Of someone running towards you,
The flash of her white dress.

Here the equilibrium between metaphor and identity is perfect, and the poem, thereby, unforgettable. The process is perfectly accounted for in another poem in Vickie Karp's remarkable book, an elegy in which she commands (or implores) herself to

Close my well-repaired eyes, open my unrepaired heart.

Such is the method of Orpheus.

Richard Howard

A Taxi to the Flame

Spark

Twenty years ago in the Catskills on a wet night,
You held a sparkler in your hands and listened to its snake hiss
As if it were a voice, an explosion of wisdom come from the wide galaxy
To tell you everything you'd ever need to grow up well.

Being human, you kept only this:
That it was a gift and an event, a dandelion of electrons
Blown free of its stem, and a way in which July 4th taught you
The magician's arrogance—*now you see it, now you don't*—of summer.

But what was the joy of a hundred tiny sparks disappearing
When you wanted them to stay?
As with all great miracles, reported or invented,
It left you something you continue to believe.

That everything, everything is a brief exchange
Between the earthly and the divine.
That you yourself are a lightning rod with
A swarm of lit questions in your hands,

Conducting a small flowering radiance
From its language of touchable flame.

Police Sift New Clues in Search for Beauty

—headline in the *New York Post*

Outside the precinct, the continents sway
In a monster wind.

A cat snoozes on a humidifier
In the corner of the squad room,

Her unfettered breath keeping time
With the office clock.

Her favorite cop glares at
The barracuda faces of wanted men

Posted in a row on the wall, their beauty
Clearly drained off, but to where?

"I did it and I'm glad," says the first face.
"I did it and I'm glad," says the next.

The Public Defender chews his lunch thoughtfully,
As if feeling for nails with his teeth.

All morning and afternoon,
He and the rookies plowed through fields

Of bluish data,
Each in his own way,

The P.D. has fears of dying, of rescuing
A maiden who crushes him with her weight and terror.

He keeps one eye on the door,
The pale glue of a tear idling beneath his lid.

2

Through the glass partition
To the captain's office, someone mutters

"I know it's here somewhere . . .
I saw it, for Chrissake!"

While slowly, against the breakers,
Evening sets sail on the East River

With its freight of passions,
As, uptown in Helsinki, her evidence

Burning gaily in the handsome fireplace,
Beauty reads her mail.

And in Caracas
Beauty plunges her hand into a book

As if to read it by touch.
And in a murky corner of Antwerp

Beauty unwraps
A heart-round box of chocolates,

Each one the dark shape of a hill,
And in Irkutsk

Beauty, bending to tie a shoe,
Lifts up her head expectantly.

Tulips: A Selected History

On your street, whose name means "roundabout" in Dutch,
The mildest weather conditions vibrate the spines of your neighbors,
Who gamble on the tulip market losing fortunes.

One gauges the sun like a bank account.
Another tastes the soils of everyone's front yards
While his dinner grows cold.

But for you, the rain has come to sound like
The dead gossiping about the dead, and you warm yourself with
The thought that evening and its underpinnings impale them all

Sooner or later, through the windows of their neat homes,
While they wake or sleep in the same chair, at odd hours,
Mistaking physical discomfort for desire.

It is the sort of night when the sky seems about to reveal its secrets.
Your wife stirs soup outdoors under the moon,
The not-so-dear orchids of garlic steaming.

She sips from an iron spoon reflecting clouds and pretends
It is a broth of your priceless *tulipa,* her dowry having all been spent
On seedlings and bulbs, drawers of fragrant possibility,

A rich man's drying room, and flower beds. She envisions
The wives of *tulipomaniacs* in Portugal, their swarthy, faceless
Husbands lugging home large bouquets of glorious colorations,

Unimaginable forms. This would needle you, of course,
But the thing to remember about women and cooking is that they do it,
As they do all things, for love.

When she frowns, as she does now,
When she looks wearily down the path where two cows are lowing
As darkness circles and drops,

It is not the chore that tires her
But the relentless composting between sweat of the real world
And ravage of the one she would make for you if she could.

Out of moon, out of water, out of whatever has gone wrong.
Never knowing it was a dream you wanted,
And that you had it all along.

A Taxi to the Flame

Halloween, I ride the subway to an early evening class
On poetry and the subconscious.

Beneath unearthly light, a man dressed as a skull and bones
Stares into the near reaches of the civilized underworld.

You would have liked the way
He politely let the living on first.

The empty seats contain a pumpkin glow, whipped
By hairs of electricity, as we shoot along at witches' speed.

A girl with a spider on her cheek reads the *Times*.
Where are we exactly?

Below 23rd. Below 14th. Below
The flat-footed beat cops and the swift commuters.

One hundred years ago; tunneling a subway
Under Boston Common, blasters uncovered shells, tools,

Even graves—an entire lateral town.
Trees, like repressed thoughts,

Were lifted out and regraded when found to be
Inconveniently deep.

A world spread its fingers under us and lifted us
Up, up by putting so much imagination beneath.

Look, I will tell my class, at the patterns in the wood
Of your desk and write down what you see:

Church spires crowded one upon the next in flat daylight,
A chorus of architecture pressed, as if into a book, of wood.

Now think of someone you've lost, someone you miss,
And tell that person about it.

I think of you and that time we took a cab to the East River Drive
To watch the Burns Brothers factory burn down.

We saw no people. No brothers. Just burning.
And behind it, a sunset repeating the pattern.

What I remembered best were the clear delineations:
The sad wobbly factory all dark and ash and lit with borrowed
menace.

The sky an anthology of color with no preface or ending,
No intention of serving as a symbol of anything.

But years later, lit by the context of your death,
I wonder about the Burns brothers.

Were they inside. Were they insured?
Did they set the fire?

And where, in tonight's sunset,
Is the piece of that flame?

Glass

At 8 P.M., each office window
Is a propped-up laboratory slide from the Mad Scientist's file.

Slide A reveals a janitor who studies the dark in a doorway,
Slide B a clutter of memos folded into hats, and there,

An executive hopeful, nearly lost in fluorescent smudge,
Who plods late into the evening, alone, for little pay—

It's Mr. X of the Department for Redundancy Department,
Another pheasant under glass for the gods.

Gray angels nibble on his window ledge—ornithology knocking
On the door of evolution—and as he reaches to pet them

His hand flattens instead on that first page of the intangible,
That portrait of physics buried in the transparent.

Dust

We find it, a motionless rage, beneath the bed.
It grows without seeming to grow,

Knitting new goods even as we stare—scouring pads
For the angels who polish forks in our dreams.

I think of an aunt who never loved anything openly,
Her remarkable sense of industry, her reverberating house

Where one could almost hear the emerald necklace of electricity
Rattling around on its clasped strand,

The minerals of hell itching under the kitchen floor.
Which ancient civilization is in this batch?

Something we can never know.
Failed brother of snow, it rises weightlessly now

Under my lamp, a brown vagabond
Made of landfill from the prairies of memory.

Harm

First, you took the parakeet out of its cage,
Its body warm and folded, a blue-green kite
With a surprised heart. Then, you scoured the metal,
The door a loose pocket of bars on two wire hinges,
The tray floor, the seed and water dishes,
The clawed perches, the swing and its endless dialogue
With the invisible. Slowly, you removed the racks
From the dishwasher and placed the cage in it.
We laughed at your ingenuity, at the way
It expressed your secret ambition to be
The cleverest, the funniest,
The one least mauled by the predictable.
And I think I knew then that I would carry on this hope
Of yours. There is such harm in love.
But let it be the green and blue acrobat it is,
A tropical danger in the midst of my body,
The body that you built for me.
Let it be the cage you cared for from which
Birdsong was pulled into the cool and colorless air.

Stars

Luminous. Ancient.
Itching to farm out a little advice.

And no shock the intergalactic patois is English,
The supportive murmur of Perseus and Cassiopeia laced with respect.

We call to them fondly from our rustic campground
For failed romantics.

Distance only adds to their pristine character
And the tango of helium to their physical charm.

One suspects the pharmaceuticals of love and hate
Are remote to them but the urgency of pain very near

And that somewhere behind those polished exteriors
Is a gilt warehouse of Cole Porter tunes.

Can they distinguish us from trees and small statues?
Or when we're prone, from park benches and snakes?

What are the odds that they care at all?
Slim, but nothing dissuades us.

All over the planet our voices rise,
Turning into ghosts and finally heat as they ascend

To that all-night café at the corner of eon and ion
Where the waitresses all look like Mom,

Where everyone forgets why he came by the time he arrives,
Like a dear old uncle out of Chekhov who borrows a cake plate

As an excuse to visit and then stays on for a meal or two,
His every complaint a code for fidelity.

Goodbye

Upstairs, a man is writing a screenplay about assassins
Who shrink to the size of pills and travel the pipes and
drains of our city,

From embassy to embassy, extinguishing conflict.
A hope derived from evenings soaking alone in a tub.

Downstairs, a solemn pair of residents called *the flesh eaters*
pack and go,
Taking their notorious dog who howled ballads from hell.

I find myself on the stoop explaining your death to an eight-year-old
Who's been storing your favorite ice cream in her freezer for weeks.

"But how will he come back?" she asks, mildly annoyed.
The sad insufficiencies of transportation drop clues all around us . . .

Not subways. Not planes. Not trucks nuzzling fenders
near the emeralds
And rubies of traffic lights. Not buses, those elephants

Of the New World, toting the moderately intrepid like
pangs of emotion,
Their sides plastered with advice.

Poor you if you've wound up in some ethereal jungle.
But, then again, poor you if heaven is too much like what
we already know:

A roadless place on a map of dust where everything vanishes without
Explanation—the capital *I* of your body laid out beneath

The uninformed chatter of leaves, cloth of your skin unweaving,
Tumbled poles of your bones, no longer animated argument of your lungs

Merely a fragrance now, and soon not even that.
Better that you go where perfect sentences take up the letters

Of your name, and the agonizing softness of what was once your weight
Becomes the tint of your unhurried soul,

While here professors of dread and remorse speak of you
Endlessly, by heart.

One Hundred Well-Cut Leaves

Please say more about the last night of your life,
How, alone on the giant white door of your hospital bed,
The exit through which you would leave forever,
You stretched out large as you could
Beneath the rubber web of life support and thought,

These are not tubes at all.
These are branches.
Each well-cut leaf a year of my life,
Falling like a gauntlet in autumn,
My body its infrangible trunk,
My hair a singed nest,
And my daughter, that tiny bird flown off
And eyeing me hungrily.

Because your wrists were tied,
Because your windpipe was burrowed into with sails of gauze,
Because you nodded yes so evenly to good and evil,
I became afraid, a dark jeweled excavation of fear.

It's terrible to think of the doctor
Pulling off those branches when you died,
The tap root through your throat and down into your lungs
Reappearing, inch by inch, like a fisherman's line
Reeled in empty.

Now as the trees in my backyard throw down their
Hundred well-cut leaves, I pick them up
And stroke their sharp edges,

Read their old Braille skins, their veins which are older
Than human veins, their stems so much more visible
Than human stems.

You will never say more about your childhood,
Your parents, the poverty, the tenacity,
About chicken farms and cheese factories,
Selling leather goods off the back
Of a station wagon, playing cards in the Catskills.

More about the Navy, your courtship of my mother,
The brother you loved who fought in the Boxer Rebellion
And kept the gray photographs, a modest vault of evil,
Beneath the bed where he slept.

You'll never say more about the cycles of things,
The giant abstract cycles that stand so tall
We cannot see all of the edges at once.

Elegy

Light on the table so capable of leaving.
Jackal of noise drifting through these rooms, scent of heat.

Think of that day you took me to the eye doctor's,
His blurry office, the shining medical charts.

What did I see when he placed a picture of a fly before me?
I saw it fly, become what it claimed to be.

Tonight, unobserved, blackness lifts you out of your grave in Florida,
Atom by atom, and translates you back through its sieve.

But I still think of you lying in the ground in street clothes,
Flowers rocketing past you through the black horizon of soil

Until they burst into blooms in the outer space which was your life.
Close my well-repaired eyes, open my unrepaired heart,

And I can feel your fingers trembling under the earth
As you try to catch them. Think, instead, of that day.

We took the ferry home.
The bent wire of a seagull's leg stirred the silence

And then an unruly alphabet of birds clamored behind the boat,
Kite of speech mimicking the air.

Your expression said let the birds have their reasons,
Let their beautiful resemblances mean less than their lives.

The Consequences of Waking

—for Howard Moss

From a fish store window, on their deathbed of ice,
A school of porgies, butterfish and smelts
Considers an elderly stroller holding a bag of shrimp.

In the layering dark, all the shops around him form a sequence
On human evolution. In the pet shop, snakes plunder
The depths of biblical fig trees.

At the dress shop, a bearded tailor clothes a human form
And sticks it, endlessly, with pins. Gloves, on sale,
Hang from invisible wire in a blue diorama,

Lit from underneath like a failed plan for stars.
Gloves point west, mittens thumb rides and palm for change,
But this the tailor doesn't see,

Nor the tableau across the street of a pale floor manager
At the *Catch A Wink Bed Boutique*
who stands between curtain and glass,
Sales pad in hand, watching the moon float.

Mattress salesmen play cards behind the grave-sized bedding
Below a reproduction of Giotto's Lazarus, who is slowly coming to,
On a calendar for MARCH.

Taking the name of the month literally, they file out together
For a trip to the health club pool, only to find a bored lifeguard
Dozing on one of the diving boards over a blue-green void.

Lined up now, annoyed, on the tiniest launch in their universe,
They bellow a schoolboy threat, catapult forwards, and jump
Into the still life of water below.

Later, when they put on their pants and shirts and go,
They pass the fish store, filled with expert swimmers, and study
As if shopping out a dream,

The silk parachutes of squid, the recluse clams,
Fifty soiled ballet slippers of sole in a heap,
A whole flounder wrapped round its precious fillet, and,

Closest to the exit, rainbow trout examining the snow
That falls like bait, like a hundred vowels
In search of a language.

On Your Birthday,
Looking through a Telescope at Jupiter

—for Tsvi Dym

From the roof of the *Good Earth* restaurant,
You peer through a telescope at the rims of stars,

Your disembodied gaze gymnastic in the dark.
Throngs of antennae stand or sit near the balustrades,

Joints chirping in the breeze as there—
In the lull of middle space—Copernicus mugs for the camera,

His face a knot of chemicals, and through it
You think you can see the moons, unimaginably apart

But synchronized, swathed in ammonia, listening to the radio
They call mother. Below, terrestrial waiters

Are ticking around the dining room, their luminous white jackets
Eclipsed by dancers, cups and saucers aloft.

And so entwined by the double music of the spheres—
Lyrics down here, melody up there—with your telescope

Lifted rifle-high at heaven or thereabout,
You begin to sweet-talk the angels back to earth,

Back into the bodies that you know,
That tell you nothing.

Tied to the Earth

Spiders type out a chapter on free will in the shade.
Dark city perennials, eight agile legs apiece,

How they ignore us, we who cannot learn their narratives.
Blue jays the color of moderate heat scream past

Like matadors, swinging the capes of their wings,
Their jet stream a riveting phrase in all the unlike air.

But spiders do not care.
Left amid the grazing violences of the everyday,

They prefer the more pastoral seductions . . .
The lingerie of Queen Anne's lace draped casually over stems,

The heavy breathing of snared prey, the ground
Stretched out beneath, round as a plate.

Nearby, the neighbor's mutt hops out a thank-you note
For decent meals routinely served,

For his own continuing story with its submerged plot
Hovering like a dogcatcher just beyond the retreating dark.

He's even managed to make friends with the wet cat
Who's hunched into a cliff on the hood of a car.

Such equanimity makes us forget
To question who we are.

Insurance

Each passing bird's a bit of punctuation thrown through the air,
And here is morning, old grammarian, descending a stair.

Let the ocean nibble at its edges.
Let the great parentheses of trees press it into shape.

To understand chaos, be chaos.
Brightness gets out of its white chair.

We know what can undo us, and we keep it where
We can see it, but what of the distance

That darkens and fills with the second thoughts of starlight,
That hangs over us every night its opulent alternatives?

Broken necklace of light, protect us from our unadorned nature,
From the slow crumbling insurance of belief,

From the diminutions that revise us and revise us,
Describing the one true gesture that we know,

The one that says, as the ocean repeated a minute ago,
Build up an argument for your life phrase by phrase.

Love is in the rewrites.
Be slow.

Watching the Commuters Read

Their postures are desultory, listing
Ever so gently to one side in order to glance

At the number of remaining pages.
Megatrends, Coma, Let's Learn Japanese . . .

One woman balances her make-up on a biography
Of Maria Callas and waves a wand of mascara

With imperious magician's strokes, as if to raise the diva
From her coffin of facts and affection.

A man has fallen asleep and looks
As if he's been shot through the heart,

A frothing copy of Louis L'Amour hitting the floor
With a small fluttering argument.

Another is so encumbered by passion,
His lips purse in a kiss

As he mouths out the consonants
Of a particularly emphatic hero.

And nearest me, a girl in spandex has put her diet book aside
And is diligently reading her tennis shoes.

Rubbed to a burnished glow on the courts
And lit now by natural light, they are Aladdin's lamps,

However demoted and adjusted for contemporary life.
And, sure enough, through the train window,

Her wishes whizz by in a comic spree—
Swimming pools and rose gardens, chubby red convertibles,

Husbands repairing things, children, puppies, even a pony
Who sails lightly through the air

Above a hurdle with a crooked sign
Proclaiming JESUS IS LORD.

No Lazarus, she nevertheless rises
Out of her seat, wincing

Not with pain but with thinking, to consider
The upcoming town in which the lawns are vast and even.

I see her whole then, a fine large fruit
Wanting to drop off its tree and ripe for the picking

By the neighborhood true crime bookshop
Where a pale, lightly freckled man with hooded eyelids

Patiently waits. Give her a whodunit, I think,
But tell her who's done it.

Give her a big fat chicken of a book
Whose every feathery phrase contains a clue

To fratricide, greed, and ruined inheritance.
For God's sake, distract her from all these houses

Showing their endings to stories never quite selected
Yet dearly paid for, their heaped-up backyards,

Their *Big Boy* tomato plants arthritic with dreaming
And frozen in the midst of great speed.

In the shaky aisle, a little future bride covets
Her mother's *Harlequin* romance—not to read it

But because it is flapping, a giant thick-winged moth
Of pages, way above her head.

Its noise interrupts, with a calm and dignified *Om*
Of chaos, the humbler power of the unopened *Hansel and Gretel*

She blithely swings from hand to hand as she jumps.
She knows the secret of reading is, after all, possession,

A benign imperialism for those of us
Who rent our hopes and adventures.

"I was lying on the sofa reading Nana," Jean Rhys whispers
Through the pages. *"It was a paper-covered book*

With a coloured picture of a stout, dark woman
Brandishing a wine glass. She was sitting on the knee

Of a bald-headed man in evening dress. The print
Was very small, and the endless procession of words

Gave me a very curious feeling—sad, excited,
And frightened. . . ."

Sad young Jean Rhys, long dead, makes me rummage around
For help by reading indiscriminately over people's shoulders.

"Think of your investments as a yo-yo going up a staircase. . . ."
"God is good. It is a beautiful night."

The whitened pages of the train window are gritty
With unreadable Braille, sooty as dextrose to the touch.

I place my hands upon them much as Gretel placed hers
Upon the candy that was nearly her doom.

The Red Dress

—for Cynthia Zarin

Some autumn leaves create a space in the shape of a red dress.
Faceless, heartless, cool where the eyes would be,
It makes an artless citizen floating sulkily

Above a pedestal of maples, an inadvertent fund of spirits
For some other planet whose weary inhabitants can't reach Earth.

There is a tiny body that lives its entire life inside our mind,
The ultimate hermit, the chaste lover who stays
For the sake of something that happened long ago, something

We originally thought little about that has had consequences,
Like a good Greek tragedy.

"That is the dress I want to wear when I die," I tell the hermit.
"When I am no longer the terrified audience,
the translator between us,
When you and I, after years of betrayals, switch places."

Still Life in the Coat Factory Office

What did you think would happen
When you got on that pale boat and

Came to America, came here to Essex Street,
Where the vibrant machinery of your heart

Is rustic compared to the hiss and boom
Of this captainless ship?

You speak to women you've never met
On the telephone, voices full of curls

And twangs thickened by the borderless
Hallucinations of long-distance wires.

Their laughter clicks and drones until
The women become nothing

But another machine you've learned how to run,
A switchboard for the bodiless voices of Georgia.

In the beginning, they squealed at
Your accent and you clucked at theirs.

You've made up a game about it—you
Pretend it's all French and elegant as lace.

A still life of the *Café de la Paix*
Hangs by one nail behind the Big Boss' desk.

In the perpetual rain, a woman sits
And stares at her leg.

27

She doesn't see the broad-chested waiter
Under the awning, but you do.

His face is a lunacy of fixed points
Painstakingly arranged in the name of art.

He's been looking straight at you for years,
Waiting to take your order.

Places You'll Never Go

—for Yehuda Mayer Dym

"Just once," he told himself in the summer of 1944,
And he tiptoed out of his hiding place on a farm in Grenoble.

He was desperate for sound. Light itself had become a conversation,
Had grown round as bronze harps and trombones.

West hissed the shining birches.
East sang the glimmering flutes behind the trapdoors of leaves.

He was caught in a café , locked in a barn, the barn set on fire.
Now we say to his children, "Long enough. Let go of it,"

Snow falling gently on the silks of their futures.
But when they look at snow, they see the handkerchiefs of the dead,

Swan-colored fragments initialed by all he'll never say.
For a year or two, his daughter searched for him.

"Maybe he was put in a camp," she said. "And he has amnesia.
And he can't find his way home." No one could stop her.

"Maybe I'll see him on the avenue or in the park," she said.
"He'll look older and thin. I won't spot him easily.

"But when I do, I'll move towards him with the greatest care,
Across these streets that he loved though he won't remember why."

How Peace, after Asking Its Question, Becomes War

During the news in the thirties, my grandmother hummed
   with symphonic sadness
For grief, for failure, and soon, cave-deep in my grandfather
   ranged a belief
Beyond the God-long expanse of plumbing, and wiring, and facts.

He'd lie down to sleep in the vanishing wilderness of his own life,
Ask the murdered to look out from that great savannah of heaven,
   where the herds increase,
And tell him how he could do anything but plough the pages
   of the *New York Herald*

With his small bone tractor of a hand. Eventually, he went to war.
Last night, upside down in my sleep, the past fell ahead of me
   like the road to a myth.
In my hand, the luminous map of the century,
   its edges held up by ghosts.

I gazed into far-off space where some man pulled cranks on
   nuclear control boards
Like Dr. Strangelove's soda-jerk son, and I saw the boots of the military
Disintegrating in the desert, yellow scorpions nuzzling up in the heels,

The heavy metal of hearts exploding, and all expressions of intent
   became desert as well,
The voice left too thirsty to even speak.
One can read and misread the textures of such a dream:

Dust settling on the brow of a commander in chief; scarlet flowering
the jaws
Of the scientists; the long human coat of the army unbuttoning.
How many times, after napping among the verbs of fantasy,

Has death risen in the real dark, with orders its only transport out?
Myth becomes nothing but its pitiful love story freed of time
   and space.
There we are, digging in our garden or sweeping up

The litter of a local violence, when war paratroops down to us as if
From a deeper dream or intelligence. Quiet as ash, it nests on our future . . .
A landscape borrowed from novelists, and a longing that rises
   in the middle of nowhere.

Part of Night

A glass of port whose ruby sequins
Jiggle and burn in lamplight
Stands untouched beside a book.

Secure the coverlet,
Secure the lamp,
Secure the dream.

The magic trick of desire
Is in its orbit,
And night rehearses a new play.

Celestial actors
Arrive in black and white,
A courtroom of love and justice.

Steam rises in a grate
And threatens to become a ghost,
Is a ghost.

Ghost of autumn.
Ghost of despair that frightened you
With its ideas.

Even the blackbird,
Who paces up and down a branch
Like an old Republican understands what you won't.

Open the curtain.
Open the window.
Open the book . . .

We had a terrible life, my brother and I.
A terrible life and it wasn't going to get any better.
He had the thinnest legs,

The boniest fingers, spigots of hair
On his conical head, on his knuckles.
It was hard to leave him alone.

I wanted a different life,
Different hair, different clothes.
I'd finish the food on other people's plates

—The reflecting soups,
The little round skins of pancakes,
The night-colored bits of meat.

Our room was depressing and we knew it.
No television. No radio. No phone.
I invented the evening news.

The headlines tended to be warnings.
He had a girl's voice. The voice of a squeeze toy.
It was so hard to leave him alone.

Bad enough to have meant well and failed, but how
To explain the well-lit unease so visible on his face
That even I could not look into it plainly?

I'd wonder about his face in the dark.
Mother's face. I began to see it everywhere,
And every morning, I floated nearer.

God never said kill him.
God merely said listen to your mother.
She misses him.

I fed his mail to the birds.
I filled his cereal with salt.
I hid his shoes.

I did not shower or speak. I did not want
To become distracted and, slowly, over months,
Time became precious to me again.

My eyes began to glow. I lifted. I lifted
Just a few inches off the ground and began to live
In a house slightly up and to the right of my real one.

A house of chaos.
A laboratory of chance for his body.
He was afraid of me.

His face would rise above us and threaten to leave.
The hair on his legs and arms began to grow.
A hillock, a pasture of flesh and wheat

Below the expressive moon.
How does Whitman say it?
The beautiful uncut hair of graves.

And so I killed him when the time was right.
And so I cut him in two
And put his head in the hallway near the milk bottles.

I knew I was being dramatic.
The effect was strong.
The face, in its terror, had turned vivid and ripe

And beneath it, I'd harvested the field.
But the harvest was not clean.
The newspapers did not say it that way.

The newspapers were a surprise.
And then the interference,
The recriminations, the fame.

34

Then the trial, the banishing,
The questions about my childhood,
The questions about my friends,
My intelligence, hobbies, dreams,
About my old girlfriends—the last I'll ever have—
And how they reacted when they'd heard.

And what of their afterlives,
Their battles with surprise, hands spread open
On the countertop to keep from falling through knowledge?

Once you do, dear friends, once you do,
Be grateful for what
You cannot feel.

Sitting on the Beach with Nachman

1

A bus has blown up in Jerusalem, #35. Nelson's bus to work.
Its black hulk sizzles at the foot of Geula Street.

Forty-six injured. Two killed. The burnt offering of a lady's handbag
Hangs by one strap on the sooty window railing.

2

Across the Red Sea, at the Gulf of Aqaba, complacent oil tankers doze
Before the triangular hills. A walkable distance were the sea to open up
  again.

Nachman follows me down to the beach, smoking a pipe in the 110
  degree heat.
Tonight, we will meet all together for the first time since the last war:

A few from the kibbutz near Qiryat Shemona, from Rosh Pinna and
  Tel Aviv,
And we, the visitors from New York City.

3

Nelson drives down from the Galilee. He offers some volunteers a lift
In his Autobianchi, across the sandy planks of the desert,

Past the U.N. vehicles white as fairy-tale sheep, past the sea-blue doors
Of the Arab houses on the West Bank, the curved moon of a hill,

Where they see the goats first, then lambs, then the wood-colored
  sheep
Of the Bedouin, an aqua hand of paint on the rams, fifty head at least,

Tired and stringy, and then the woman plowing through the powder
Of sand and sunset, her husband behind her on a burro.

"Look!" say the volunteers. And Nelson says, they tell us later,
"She doesn't walk behind him anymore. She walks ahead in case of
    mines."

4

"When I came to Israel," Nachman tells me, "I was in the Merchant
    Marine.
In Glasgow, they said marry and settle down. So I did. Then I went to
    China.

"I wandered the Near and Far East, came to Jerusalem, then north to
    the throat
Of the Galilee. Spent eleven years working in the fish ponds.

"Once got my arm opened up by the smack of a St. Peter's fish.
'Lucky it was your arm,' they told me.

"The wars change you, of course. At night, I'd take my bottle, stand in
    the groves,
And recite the Song of Solomon to an audience of avocados.

"I went off somewhere in Africa once to calm my nerves.
Not far from Mozambique, a gang of white boys

"Laddered a kiddie's swimming-pool slide with razor blades.
Couldn't see the silver blades through the silver water.

"The first child down was a pudgy boy of eleven, soft and black as
    rubber.
He shrieked like he was winding his way through hell.

"My baby!" screamed his mother. "Not my baby!"

5

Radio news at the Shalom café. "The *Fatah*," an American translates
for his wife,
"Has tried to blow up Eilat."

The Moroccan bartender with the milky eye
Dries the same glass over and over.

"Filled a freighter with rockets and plastics. Caught them one hundred
kilometers
Off the beach. Had to sink the boat."

His son waves a fork of spaghetti for attention. He is pleased with the
suspense
And wiggles his arms. Tomato sauce, red as blood, on his face.

6

Red beach. Red sky tacked up by stars. I put on sneakers and wade out
Among the little black needles of the sea urchins.

The Moroccan bartender rolled his eyes and bet the waiter
I would not make it to the reef.

A few feet in, the water clicks open and shut like metal.
Nachman is poking around the shore with a stick.

I feel my veins lightening with breath.
I think of all the ways we could get hurt, just like this.

Boat

You who lives out behind that mountainous region
Of apprehension that cuts us each in half, how
Do you come here, to the part of the body which is our earth,
The unclothed face and hands of a dark universe?

Last night, on a schooner in Buzzard's Bay,
I drank coffee and thought about this.
The sweet-faced dog slept on his imagined prey,
Long legs of land stepped over us

Making so much of this life seem invisible,
A hole in the deep pockets of death.
Morning rolled out like a coin spent on time and space.
I curled into the boat of my body and sailed

Back into my heart to steal something from it,
Or perhaps just to look. I traveled the corridors
Of my veins like a pirate, and the terrorist in me
Kicked at the moon.

The Juniper Bonsai

It rests on tiny roots, a vision of angles,
And lives long.

It has no passion for gossip and little need for the usual,
Yet craves aftermath.

Likes to drink simply. Holds up its arms as directed
Yet does not harvest bitterness.

Is increasingly valuable with age.
Would not pay so much for itself.

Teaches quality through the distilled masterwork
Of each leaf, through its accurately expressed trunk.

Is beyond the concept of seasons as loss.
Measures in minutes and sees years as a form of belief.

Prefers suggestion: humidity for rain, admiration for ownership,
A firm pot instead of the earth itself.

Contains a noise of emotion in its resistance
Rather than in its growing.

Does not like to be touched without motive.
Does not ask which sorrow will fell us,

Will shrink us into a single gesture
So that one or two may deny that we are gone at all

By using our very lumber to make man-made shapes
Of our original unarticulated selves,

Even as we stand,
Even as we live.

The Neighborhood Environmental Center

In front of the aquarium of frowning garter snakes, plump crabs,
And snouted fish of the North Shore, Art is gossiping
With Hope.

"You're pretty," he yells out the back door
To cross-country skiers gliding by in pastoral target practice.
"Useless, but very pretty."

He turns into the room where sacks of birdseed, open on the floor,
Rise and fall on a glistening beach of corn kernels and grains.
His son explains the wood-burning stove to visitors.

Posed a polite distance away, we study the shiny shells of the turtles,
Their soft drunken smiles, the way they seem to dream of the creek
Only a few walls away, half frozen now, beside which the woodcutter

Runs ripply trunks down the length of a log splitter
As if he were bowling, and where shorebirds watch the sun set
In a batch of tulip trees over the Belt Parkway.

And there, past the long odd hill in the scabby marsh—a snow-covered
    sewer pipe
Neatly sketched with the tracks of pheasant and raccoon—fresh and
    salt water
Blend and unblend in native square dance.

There, a mud wave created by a man who used old cars for landfill.
It's a road to nowhere now for the winter flounder, the bay anchovy,
The whiting, all our Martian-far relations,

Including the Army Corps engineer here on mud wave investigations
Who conducts the evening tide sweeping up now and running,

Running after the pointed finger of the moon's ray.
Soon it will point at us.

Getting Dressed in the Dark

June, yet the roses are still asleep in their black dormitory.
Illusions of grandeur dissolving mid-air, like sugar in weak tea.

Soon, they will hoist themselves out of their despair,
Muscling in on the atmosphere with their fragrant animosity.

The hedge-clipper's bicycle, a pair of spectacles at this distance,
Leans against some reticent shrubs.

For blocks, the lawns are strewn with tattered burlap.
Brown, stained with the sweat of dew, it could be clothing

Tossed from your dreams, the entire wardrobe
Of your dread unconscious pitched out

As your body, the quivering pelt, slept on
Clad only in bracelets of air.

In the bedroom, surrounded by four-legged non-creatures
—Table, chair, dresser, bed—

The body rises, shifting its inner tropic from swamp to tree,
Pats the floor for its shoes, places a thumb

On each side of a sock—the mugging grin of a boy
About to stick out his tongue—

And slowly, as if dipping a foot into cold water,
Rolls the puddle up over each ankle.

Upright now, wrapped in a drape
By the window, see the bit of cloth

With flaps like arms that lies chest down
On the neighbor's lilac?

A pale shirt? A smoking victim from that night you thought
You were Deianira in a world without a doting Heracles?

Soon, the red velvet she might have found to enchant him
Without killing him will hang at the top of every ladder of thorns.

The Lost Lover

Look at how, on the broad silk of that river,
The moon drops its skins as it moves.

Thin as heat, they twist among reflected trees,
Safe for a moment, then pulled apart by water.

Now, another woman enters your room each night
And you find your way of turning all the way in

To her body without leaving what you already have
Inside yourself.

In my sleep, the oaks
Shake their heavy hands free of her.

I stand up, the white chrysanthemums
Of the pillows falling away.

And on my back is the sketch of that tree, a sparrow-thin net
Of branches where your hands rested.

Driving Home

New month.
The birds turn once around
On the fence and you look
At October as if it were made
Out of copper.

There is fog on the thruway.
A tattered kite strewn
Through the long fingers
Of a maple.

Another mile and it is the kite
You lost years before.
A wild dog barks in the doom
That's settled behind what
You remember.

Three more hours of watching
Your hands as if they were
The last two leaves of autumn.

The mountains rise and turn,
Like the past raising
Its broad back.

Winter and Its Steps

Once again, winter calls for itself with both hands
Folded behind its back, its eyes cast like dice.

Half hidden already, we'll retreat further
Into our house and then into the catacombs of our nerves,
The ghosts of guilt.

You'll peer into the threat of your own face
As if you were shaving.

I'll play the piano for an audience
Of photographs stretched like stars across the spinet.

And the forest will seem to recede, leaving behind
A raft of logs on which to sail out of this season each evening.
What are you looking for

In the portraits of your mother sitting in a high-backed chair,
Your father whose eyelids are eternally lowered into two smiles?

All around us, sparrows cut the crops of ice and evergreen
With their shadows.

On the Satin Virtues of Milk

From your car, you see the cows swerve out of the way
Of an oncoming wind. Their watering hole quietly breathes.

Their copse of trees parts its hair. Why not stop
And watch the air settle down upon its ruminating loom,

Watch the cows whose eyes light routes leading everywhere,
Routes you will never travel if not now?

Their flanks are a gallery of islands. On one, you see yourself
Watching television with the dog as it steals your cup of milk.

It drinks so softly. Little kisses, really,
That whisper a message of gratitude through the satin

As its black face sinks and rises,
Covered in white.

Endless Greetings

After years of painting no black, no gray, you experience a dream of
    destiny.
Thin parades of your peers in frock coats and coal-dark hats
Spell out a sentence of welcome that will outlive you.

Slippers whispering, they walk through your bedroom in Rouen,
    which is
Floodlit now with felicity, past your young wife, who is alive again
And leaning against the doorway in a great silver C, the hollows

Of her starved cheeks filled out with evening air.
Your palettes, flat as spilled beer, granulate in this light.
In a chipped plate on the table, the shallow rosettes rise and waver.

On they go, past you to Giverny, where you will sit one day
With your steadied heart before that steady bridge. Purple. Lavender.
And farther down, the closed eyes of the lilies.

Willows lock together in subtle comradery. Light breaks from cloth
And turns to pale suggestion. And then the lilies slide apart in curtains
Of pink and yellow humus, rich brown.

Now a green smoke rises.
An underwater bursts up and spreads its mackerel skin.
The white rings of birch spin in solitude.

The fragrance of the bank infuses the anticipation
Of someone running towards you,
The flash of her white dress.

The Powers of Time and Space

—for Lynne Fried

Sunset. Who knows what I don't see on its bridge
Of color that bends back into light the way a man bends
Back into himself each night when he goes to sleep.

The clouds clamp shut, and darkness falls down on us.
A hatless man leans on his ax in the middle
Of a field, grass sinking in darkness.

Did he feel the eyes on his back when he left his home, left
His youth, crossed over the wooden planks of despair and let
The old man step out of him where none of the family would see?

How long did he stand in front of the split wood
Of his first choice, leaning on his blade as if it were
The glittering handle of something that he had to have?

It's difficult every night to walk through the dead
Brown lot of a real life, the alley cluttered with onions
And cats, with so much memory that you can hear

The children in your heart singing like broken saws,
Song of your mother saying goodbye every morning.
As you fall farther and farther out of her sight,

She raises the blind high as if waving goodbye forever.
How could anyone know what resemblances
You'd find looking back years later

From the rim of one life to another,
Her half-pulled curtain and yours forming congruent triangles
Across open space.

Dark Blue Ribbons
under the Streets of the City

The streets are melting into promises
And recreating themselves out of glass and ice,
Out of glints of ancient sediments
And fumes of asphalt.
Their music is the eruption of footsteps,
The ringing of coins, the thrum of black tar,
Gray chips and brown fissures.
The cracking and breaking of things as they are.
Underneath, deep, deep beneath reason, where the heart
Is a cast of thousands, all lost, all moving,
Rivers of possibility shift back and forth under lamplight
And hope is a spectator with a certain amount to bet.
Bet on the days to come—racehorses flush with promise.
Sure-footed, untried, they kick and fuss at the gate
Of the new year, the dark blue ribbons of their manes
Flying out behind them like the ice-blue streets.
I can see the most beautiful
Off in the distance of white buildings and glazed water towers,
Carrying nothing on its back, barely touching the ground.
And I say to it what I always say to the future . . .

Begin again. Begin again.

The James Dickey Contemporary Poetry Series
Edited by Richard Howard

Error and Angels
Maureen Bloomfield

Ripper
Carl Jay Buchanan

Portrait in a Spoon
James Cummins

The Land of Milk and Honey
Sarah Getty

All Clear
Robert Hahn

A Taxi to the Flame
Vickie Karp

Growing Back
Rika Lesser

Lilac Cigarette in a Wish Cathedral
Robin Magowan

Traveling in Notions: The Stories of Gordon Penn
Michael J. Rosen

United Artists
S. X. Rosenstock

The Threshold of the New
Henry Sloss

Green
Sidney Wade